I LOVE YOU, MOM!

13-Digit ISBN: 978-1-40034-080-4
10-Digit ISBN: 1-4003-4080-2

This book may be ordered by mail from the publisher. Please include $5.99 for postage and handling. Please support your local bookseller first!

Books published by Cider Mill Press Book Publishers are available at special discounts for bulk purchases in the United States by corporations, institutions, and other organizations. For more information, please contact the publisher.

Cider Mill Press Book Publishers
"Where good books are ready for press"
501 Nelson Place
Nashville, Tennessee 37214

cidermillpress.com

Typography: Greycliff CF, Salthouse

Image Credits: Vectors used under official license from Shutterstock.com.

Printed in Malaysia

24 25 26 27 28 OFF 5 4 3 2 1
First Edition

I LOVE YOU, MOM!

A BOOK MADE
JUST FOR YOU

BY: _____

CIDER MILL
PRESS

BOOK
PUBLISHERS

HERE'S A PORTRAIT OF YOU:

I DREW IT MYSELF!

ONE OF MY FAVORITE MEMORIES OF YOU IS...

_____

_____

_____

_____

_____

_____

_____

_____

_____

_____

YOU ARE
ONE OF
A KIND!

I ALWAYS HAVE FUN
WHEN WE GO...

_____

_____

_____

_____

_____

_____

_____

_____

_____

_____

I LOVE READING WITH YOU.
SOME OF MY FAVORITE BOOKS
WE'VE READ TOGETHER ARE...

1 _____

2 _____

3 _____

4 _____

5 _____

HERE'S A PICTURE OF MY FAVORITE THING THAT YOU COOK:

You make the best days even better!

IF I COULD GO ANYWHERE IN THE WORLD WITH YOU, WE'D TAKE A DREAM TRIP TO...

_____

_____

_____

_____

_____

_____

_____

_____

_____

YOU GIVE THE BEST ADVICE.
I'LL NEVER FORGET WHEN YOU TOLD ME...

_____

_____

_____

_____

_____

_____

_____

_____

_____

I got this
bouquet
of flowers
for you!

IF YOU WERE AN ANIMAL, YOU WOULD BE...

_____

AND THIS IS WHAT YOU'D LOOK LIKE!

IF I HAD TO DESCRIBE YOU
IN JUST FIVE WORDS,
I WOULD SAY YOU'RE...

1 _____

2 _____

3 _____

4 _____

5 _____

You give the best cuddles!

YOUR MOST AMAZING TALENTS ARE...

_____

_____

_____

_____

_____

_____

_____

_____

_____

IF YOU WERE A SUPERHERO,
YOUR NAME WOULD BE...

_____

AND THIS IS WHAT YOU'D LOOK LIKE!

YOU'RE MY FAVORITE SUPERHERO!

IF I COULD GIVE YOU ANY GIFT, HERE'S WHAT IT WOULD BE:

I GOT YOU A COUPON— IT'S A SPECIAL PROMISE FROM ME TO YOU! GOOD FOR:

☐ **One free bear hug**

☐ **A dance party with me as the DJ**

☐ **A long walk together**

☐ **Your favorite drink delivered to your seat**

☐ _____

☐ _____

☐ _____

☐ _____

☐ _____

I DREW YOU BREAKFAST IN BED
WITH ALL YOUR FAVORITE FOODS!

I MADE YOU
THIS BOOK
TO SHOW YOU
HOW AMAZING
YOU ARE!

MOST OF ALL,
I LOVE YOU BECAUSE...

_____

_____

_____

_____

_____

_____

_____

_____

_____

I LOVE YOU,

_____

ABOUT CIDER MILL PRESS BOOK PUBLISHERS

Good ideas ripen with time. From seed to harvest, Cider Mill Press brings fine reading, information, and entertainment together between the covers of its creatively crafted books. Our Cider Mill bears fruit twice a year, publishing a new crop of titles each spring and fall.

"Where good books are ready for press"
501 Nelson Place
Nashville, Tennessee 37214

cidermillpress.com